Follow the White Rabbit

Poetry to Portal With

Follow the White Rabbit

Poetry to Portal With

Some of these poems first appeared in We Are One and Know Your Way chapbooks; Cosmic Civilization: E-Zine V3 and Day of Poetry 1997, University of Pittsburgh.

Front cover photo credit to Gibran Larbi, 2023.

Back cover art by Sarah Mauri, 2023.

First edition.

Published by Four Wild Geese Design, Mount Shasta, California 96067

ISBN 978-1-7324373-4-0

Dedicated
to those
Doorways
Sacred Symbols
Crop Circles, Geometry, Numerology
Showing us the way.
Gateways,
Open doors
Portals
into mystery.

Preface

Whenever there is a strong sense of community, collaboration happens. I am blessed to be a part of such a community in Mount Shasta, California.

Follow the White Rabbit contains poetry, prose and art from many including myself. Credit is given throughout the book, and on the copyright page for the front and back cover contributions.

The white rabbit is a strong symbol in modern mythology. Even more so, for 2023, being the Chinese year of the rabbit. The rabbit says 'Follow me', going beyond your comfort zone; your home, hutch, or rabbit hole.

Be open to new experiences---and you will receive blessings.

An old wives tale for prosperity goes as follows. On the first day of the month, rub peppermint on your doorstop while repeating 'white rabbits'. Doing so, will invite good fortune and expanding states of consciousness in.

I encourage you to leap forward, and find the magic that works for you.

"Imagination is more important than knowledge. It embraces the entire world not just what we know." Albert Einstein

...imagination is the very gateway of reality...Neville Goddard

Table of Contents

Contributors and Author pages

Alchemy
through Yeshardo

Stimulate the radicals
Perma-sabbaticals
Navigate the rabbit holes
Angels come in intervals

Cultivate prosperity
feel it in the body
speak up with sincerity
raise vibes in life's lobbies

Emancipate the belly laugh
chuckle, grin and chortle
huffing all that laughing gas
2 another portal

So regulate those endocrir es
spend dopamine wisely
sort thru all the synonyms
articulate precisely

Fluctuate the repertoire
stirrup all those neurons
agitate the reservoir
scrape the lake like her-ons

Conjure up a cozmic duck
waddle thru tha murk n gunk
wade around, dip and dunk.
Flap them wings n waft your funk.

I Am by Cheryl

In the cosmos, I am
a Solar Quartz--
shimmering, sparkling.

My blinding starlight
brings healing, love and
synchronicity.

I shine mauve, orange and
lavender-- all at once.

I smell like cinnamon and
sassafras tea.

I run like a black equine---
Secretariat.

I hobnob my way to write
poetry at the cattywampus!

Portal by Cheryl

Feeling gratitude and awe
for this next step.
We are on the cusp
of a Big Leap.

Who else feels it?
The excitement is in the knowing.
We have made it.
Give thanks to all your helpers.

I'm like a child's balloon filled with helium---
that needs held onto.
Catch it
Or,
let go--
Fly.

Slip thru the eye
of the needle.
Come out on the other side.
Portal.

Children of the Sun by Cheryl

The god of ale
came to me and said
'take a whiff'
'have a sip'
You are a winner--
take a bow--
claim your prize--
a trip to the dome.

The dome shines, sparkles--
a golden Sun god.
Surya.

Children of the Sun---
Open your eyes
and see,
a secret message.

The Horizon---
holds the Key--
secrets lay
between the lines
spaces
ley lines--

Stepping
on earth grids,
We ignite the way
sparkle and shine
for all to see--
like a vein of gold
rising to the surface
hot lava
streaming---forging
new trails.

4

Figments of Divinity's Imagination
by Damiel Balderrama

Dive deep into the pineal fractal.
Explore the space that isn t a place,
where you may observe the unseen,
and witness the presence
of no thing in every thing.
If you can't see it, just make it up.
We're making it all up anyway.
If you can't unsee it,
then you know you're there,
in that space that isn't a place.
Where your memories of the future
are figments of Divinity's imagination.
There, you and I...can sit together
in the screening room of eternity.
Watching reruns of the source code.

Comets by Cheryl

Watch Out---
Hailey's coming home.

You may feel loopy---want to cry---have a dumb stare
But don't fret--
It's all part of the plan.

On the eve---
take a peek---
It's jaw dropping--
Gasp inspiring.

A real treat.

Like the Green Lantern---
ZTF zooms by--

Healing
our hearts, minds and souls.

Glimpses by Cheryl

Beauty visits me
cold and quiet
early morning

Feeling the connection of
all I have ever experienced,
witnessed--
Watching with acceptance and detachment--

Leaving---
going to no time or place

But
arriving
all at once.

RIP
Douglas Peter Mauri
April 6, 1956 - May 22, 2022

Becoming the Beast
by Cody Ray Richardson

Spiritual awaking or physiological break?

Both appear with similar symptoms.
Any hyper religious or spiritual person would be described as
schizophrenic.
 It's in the description that if you think your environment itself is
speaking to you through God your schizophrenic.
 I stared Into the Fire so long I could see and feel only it.
 It's pure Elemental dimension.
The fire is forever.
You can never burn the flame.
The flame devours and cleanses all.
Finally my friend grabbed me and he said get out of there.
 I was literally climbing into a physical fire.
Then I ran into the woods.
I ran and ran.
Clothes came off.
No reason to sleep.
I talked to the mountains.
The mountains spoke to me.
I buried myself in the Earth.
The watchers could not see me when I became one with her.
I witnessed reality being rebooted.
The program has to be looped.
You can notice it if you pay attention.
The whole time chasing something but not sure what I was chasing.
I could see another realm in the distance.
There was a darkness to it.
I knew somehow if I went into it I would cross over.
I would never be able to return.
It called to me.
Come live with us in our eternal realm it beckoned.
Songs of sirens.
I knew better somehow.
One track kept leading me toward it.
The other away from it.

Then after 4 days on my feet I came upon two creatures.
There were two different tracks I had been following.
At that moment they became one.
There stood a red stag before me.
Next to it was a white rabbit.
The stag on the right.
The rabbit on the left.
The White Rabbit spoke.
Put your clothes back on.
Your being ridiculous.
They should lock you up and throw away the key.
Get a job and stop being a hippie.
What was this anyway?
Some type of spiritual awaking?
Said the white rabbit.
What do you expect to find?
Then the red stag spoke.
It's voice overpowered the rambling of the white rabbit.
It said that before I was a human I was a four-legged.
I was a stag.
Then I became curious of the two legged.
I wondered what they were and why they had came to earth.
Why they were so violent.
They attacked our mother with relentless greed.
I knew I had to find out their intention.
Their soul.
Their purpose.
The only way to really know would be to become one.
I would become a human.
I would change things from the inside.
I would enter the lair of the beast by becoming one. I decided to eat
the Amanita. The powerful Amanita medicine had transformed me
into a human. The red stag said you can always come back if you eat
the Amanita again.
One day I'm going to stop listening to the white rabbit.
I will listen to the red stag and go back from Once I came.
Until then I'm going to find out what this two legged life is all about.
Real change happens from the inside.

Return to Beauty
by Cheryl

What does beauty mean to you?
Is beauty, as they say 'In the eye of the beholder'?
Can we truly judge what is beautiful?

The other day,
a male turkey crossed the road in front of me,
he strutted and sang the whole time.
In effect saying---
Be like me! Strut your stuff! Fan your tail!
Walk like an Egyptian!
Joseph wore a coat of many colors.
We all wear many coats.
He was hated by his brothers
because they deemed him the favorite.

There are no favorites!

We all are---
Shining, Exploding, Becoming,
Returning---

We will not need clothes, cars or passports!
Open UP---
It is time!

Grandmother Tree
Stands
Straight and Tall,
an example
for all of us.

We all are----Beauty.
Shining, Exploding, Becoming,
Returning.

10

A Good Time for Tea
by Crystal Scarlett

Leaves are falling and weather is crisp,
preparing us for cosmic energy shifts!
When sudden winds of change are blowing,
there's a way to keep the good vibes flowing...
A Cup of Tea! It's all you need! At Welcome Om,
yes indeed!

Tea tastes better when enjoyed with friends

Limbo

Mysterious Mountain
Heaven Meets Earth
Paradise or Purgatory

Spirit Train

Flame train blazes
Across mountain land
Delivering endless spirit

Peace Garden by Cheryl

In the garden of peace
circle of Aspen
cathedral

maze of lavender
pilgrims walking in circles
meaning in the spaces

Chaos Into Art
by Cody Ray Richardson

No straight line to my destination.
The overwhelming piles gather.
I kick through them.
Things build up.
I wonder what purpose they have.
Each has a place.
Sometimes I'm sure where they will end up.
Most of the time I have no clue.
I regret after throwing certain things away.
When creativity hits me like an asteroid.
I'm happy I have them.
I use them for what I need.
The chaos becomes art.
So interesting how they knew what they were meant for.
Even when I didn't.
They were patiently waiting.
Knowing what they would become.
Destined to be a beautiful piece of art.
Something useful for people.
Laughing as I run around.
They are more useful than me.
They know it.
Artists come and go.
They are forever.
Mad scientist.
From an outsiders perspective seeming insane.
Then boom alchemy.
Gold out of iron.
The gold was always there.
It just needed what I could provide.
A little love and elbow grease.
Nothing is ever finished to the artist eye.
It can be maddening.
The whole world looks askew.
Always something to adjust.
A brush here a piece of something there.
Thank the fathers of invention for duct tape.
Take a note out.

Add a base here.
Maybe a violin.
It needs more purple.
Oh what a wonderful experience.
What an amazing playground.
Witnessing Creativity and Technology fall in love over and over again.
Oh what beautiful children will they have next?
Creativity is Queen.
Technology is King.
We are all their children.
Nature provides the art supplies.
They are my greatest love.
Their love created me.
I will continue to turn the chaos into composition.
The piles into paintings.
The dirt into structure.
Look upon me and judge my dirty hands.
Stare and laugh.
I'm laughing all along.
A child in a wonderful playground.
I'll turn whine into water and walk upon it.
One day I hope you understand.
We will all swim together.
In a land of edible color.
The way I see it.
The way we all should.
The darkness is the canvas the light paints upon.
Come paint with me and laugh like children waking in a lucid dream.
Because that is the reality.
May life be your blanket.
May you be sponsored by love.
May your piles turn into projects.
May you see the best in everything.
Good vibes your way.

Have fun!

Art Knows by Cheryl

The yin and yang of our heart---
can be found--

in the buzz of a bee
the stripes of a zebra
and the colors of a sunset.

At---
the end of a rainbow
the point of an arrow
the curve of a circle---

There is an intersection
a special place
where we find
more--
A doorway---
                    passage---
Entry point to a new dimension---
Where energy and mass are all the same---
Some call it-- zero point, the event horizon, the aurora.

They say 'Time is Art'
I say there is no time---
only a place where beauty is waiting
to be found
and become someone's art.
Discovery.

Art is a wise woman.
She already knows.
Waiting for us to find her---
like peace
She is available to all.

Healing by Cody Ray Richardson

Honor the subtle spaces in between.

There would be no music without rests.

Intelligence is the ability to know the difference.

Without space there is no detail.

Everything will cling together void of pause.

A master was once asked what is the most difficult skill.

Teleportation is easy he replied. Invisibility not so hard.

To truly listen is the most difficult and useful skill.

Listen without response, truly be there.

I've found this to be difficult in my mortal life.

To let situations simmer.

To let them grow in their own time.

Relationships are like bread.

They need time to rise.

Time does not heal wounds.

We do, given time.

Fly Free by Cheryl

Round and Round
We go---

swirl, whirl, twirl

Take your turn.

I am the marble in the Roulette wheel---
Circling.

I am a pebble in the whirlpool.

Take your turn.

Turn dirt into pearls.

I Am a pearl.

Go thru the furnace---come out,
all shiny and new---
Phoenix.

Fly Free--
unencumbered by others ideas, expectations, demands.

"Don't throw your pearls to swine."

My trip to Maui by Cheryl

I saw a Hawaiian man
snag a baby octopus
with glee---
and claim it for his dinner.

White, well dressed
tourists
were clapping.
(I felt bad for the octopus.)

Feeling
the sadness
of separation.

My friend invited me
to stay with her in Maui.
When I wouldn't transport her
all the places she wanted to go---
I was told to leave.

"Players love you when they're playing."
If I'm not of immediate benefit to you---
then I'm not needed.

Time and Space---No.
I will not become part of this matrix.
I will not be
self absorbed or self promoting.
To me
it is ugly.

I feel sadness
at the facade---
pretend friendships
to gain something---
sales, popularity, fame---
18

It is a fixed game
anyway.
Those who lose---
gain the traits needed--
humility, compassion, acceptance
Nothing---
is as it seems.

You cheated someone
out of a seat, a dollar---
You are not winning---
You are isolating yourself---
Feeding the lie
of separation---
Prolonging the suffering.

It's all
take, take---
What can you do for me?
So sad.
Where are the open-hearted ones?
They all have their hand out.

Feeling
the sadness
of separation.

Beyond the barbwire fence--
Fruit lies on the ground spoiling.
Please let me see the end of barbwire.
No more fences, gates or keycodes.
Beyond the gates---
there is freedom.

"Pay no mind to the person behind the curtain."
It is you.

Li goes on a Trip by Cheryl

With a fin made of pine,
Li took a dive--
The dune was deep--
there he peered
a sub roaring thru goo
like an ailing train, squealing.

He reached a node,
a secure zone--
fir and pine logs dealt like craps.
A bee was having a jaw with a titmouse--

Feeling ail and crawly,
Li decided--
that roach he had at the rave earlier
wasn't quite what he expected---
So, he caught the next train home.

Spiders in the Bathroom by Cheryl

I am told Spider is a messenger and
be open to receive----

But damn---
not when I'm laying naked in a hot tub of water---
not with my pants down either--

Time and Place---
Kinda important---
In this reality----

Is it a good time?
Where can we meet?
Make an appointment---
Can you make it?
Will this work for you?

I'm not the spirit I used to be---
I can't just fly
like 1,2,3.

Gear up
to go out---
Knee wraps, ankle brace and shoes that are
slip proof--
Layers and layers of clothes---
On they go---
Off they come, sometimes in the store.

Our outsides
match our insides---
Many layers.

In the summer,
it is no different---
lightweight jacket, sunscreen, hat for shade---
sandals so my feet can breathe.

21

Animals have it better---
no trying on clothes or shoes---
to see if they fit.
Already prepared---
with their coat and shoes.

They wear no crystals for protection---
Theirs is all around them.

The rock, plant and animal kingdoms are family---
They exist peacefully.
They don't dig holes
to gather and collect---
to horde the gifts of Gaia.

Crystals are living beings---
talk to them---thank them.

Ever watch, The Lorax by Dr. Seuss---
everyone needs a thing-a-ma jig.
Not me---
"I speak for the trees."

Do like the Native Americans did,
take what you need and leave the rest.

I think the message from Grandmother Spider is---
Co-exist peacefully.
Respect all life.
Remember your ancestors.
If you come across a feather, rock or tree---
Ask the spirits before you take.
These things are sacred.
Don't use them for personal gain.
Take only what you need.
Talk to the rocks, trees and animals---
they are representatives of the Divine.

Oil & Water by Cheryl

Imagine a reality where the trees talk to you---
The giving tree---
Its said "You get what you give".

A New world---
where all is shared---afterall,
everything we have is a gift from the universe.

My learning will be
primal, natural, eternal.
The forest is my guru.

Look to the elders---
they carry wisdom bundles---
like a cord of wood--
Do they charge a special price---
$144 for a bundle?

The teachings are clear--
like water--
The cost or fee is like oil---
not clean.
Clouds up the clear.
Oil and water don't mix.

Church and State.
Step away from the matrix.

The sacred way has all but become polluted with commerce---
It is not needed.
There is another way.

Physical cost is for physical things.
Sacred things are a gift.

Ask your ancestors---
talk to the masters--
how to move into the new
5D Earth?

Live a new way
by
remembering the old ways.

Let go of the belief--
there must be a gift for a gift--
Become light as a feather
in your giving.
The exchange will be your freedom.

What holds you back keeps
this reality in place.
What are you holding onto?

The indigenous know
not to charge
for what is sacred.

Our ancestors are waiting for us---
give up the bone.

Be open to new ways
of doing, thinking, and living.
Ask yourself--
What is the next best step?
Do that.
Step by step--
we gain our
freedom and victory!

Ancient by Jennifer Hershelman

Singing to the tree--
the words, ancient and deep
from another time,
nearly forgotten, hidden, asleep.

Suddenly,
everything shifts, merges and converges.

Now,
I'm sitting in the tree,
feeling it become me.
When I open my eyes,
I'm touching the sky
The wind blowing through me as leaves on the tree
totally and utterly free.

I flow to the ground
traveling through roots
reaching out,
as far as the eye can see--
energy all connected, intertwined and integrated.

The black hills grass giggled and tickled above
as I flow through roots below.

I feel the wind again,
russling and tussling
as the Buffalo I saw a mile back
now,
stands over and on me.
Grass is a hive mind,
each blade blows singularly and together.
They giggle harmoniously.
The wind tickled
as we giggled and waved
loving to be swayed.

25

For a brief moment,
I feel myself rise
and see through Buffalo eyes.

Then snap,
I'm back at the tree
feeling my body, all around me
my feet planted in dirt.
Standing in sunshine,
bees singing to me.

Now,
time to move along.
Nothing can go wrong.
Time to help people live,
pure, connected and free.

Travels by Cheryl

Looking inward
I see the next
Rung
on the ladder of my life.

What does your Inner Spiral look like?
Black cast iron
or
a white marble staircase---

"Step by Step, we climb
to Freedom and Victory"

Ever climb trees, growing up?
Limb after limb---
So exciting
Seeing how far you can go---

Look at this life
like one Big Tree---

We are all in different places
on our climb---

Following different paths
to the top---

There's a saying---
"That's where they are."
It's not a literal place.

More like
a concept, an idea
to wrap your mind around.

So---
In our minds there are
places to go to---
that we can visit---
take a trip---

"In my Father's house, there are many abodes."

Memories---
Go down memory lane.

How often do you visit the past?
Where do you $pend your time?

Are you a time traveler,
or
a dimension/space jumper?

Be a Visionary---
See the reality
you desire.

Leap---
to the next timeline.

Know it.
See it---
in your minds eye
Then
Feel it---
in your heart.
Full of Joy.

Remembering Me by Heather Brook

In the depths of my being,
I reconnect with my soul,
Embracing the divine within,
My self-love becomes whole.

I will court myself with reverence,
Nurturing every aspect of my being,
Admiring the beauty of my spirit,
Feeling the ecstasy of truly seeing.

I will study the secrets of the universe,
As they reside within my heart and mind,
Taking care to cultivate my inner light,
So that my spirit may be truly aligned.

With each breath, I take,
I tap into the power of the cosmos,
Pulsating with the energy of creation,
Manifesting my desires and all that I know.

I am a vessel for divine energy,
A reflection of the universe's infinite grace,
In this love for myself, I become a magnet,
Attracting all that resonates with my sacred space.

So, let me always remember,
To honor the divinity within me,
For in loving myself, I become a channel,
For the universe's magick to flow through me.

What Now? by Cheryl

Don't fight it---
you'll only sink
Quicker--
Quicksand.

Up a creek
without a paddle--

Down a narrow, winding
road---
No room to turn
Around.

What now?

I am lost
in the maze of life.

Reached a dead end---
At the Final stop sign.

What now?

The tide is high---
Stay above water.
"Just keep swimming."
Grab a life line, preserver or
anchor.

This board called
Life--
is changing---
            sliding---
      into something
else.

30

What now?

Shut your eyes---
Be still---
Calm,
Center---

The answer you are seeking
is within.
"You've had it
all along."

Cataclysmic Creation by Cheryl

This explosive event is not the end all.
Earth shakes, quakes--

Woe, when mice weep.
Wink at the coming of the end of time.

Dine on your fear--
chew it up
spit it out.

Take it in stride--
Keep riding.
Be a 'Low Rider'.
Ride out the storm--
Big Bang.
'Riders of the Storm'
Thunderbirds.

Soar Free
like a flame--
Be the fire.

Lead.
Leaders lead.
Leaders of the pack.

Soul by Cheryl

See that little black spot by the sun today?

It's my soul out there,
Searching for a way home.

I am a dove---cast out
of Noah's Ark.

Hunting
for a branch of my own.

Jumbled feelings and memories
glide by--
briefly--
not long enough--
to get--
a foothold.

Same old thing as yesterday.

The impermanence of it all.

My mind is a sentry--
guards against,
lies, traps, and endless detours.

My soul longs for home.

Home by Cheryl

Death is the Door---
sail away
the Highway to Heaven.

'Halt'
There is a tin man
guarding the door.
Hire the liars---
their story will make you gasp.
It was leaked--
Can we trust it?
Don't believe everything you hear.

Roam the room.
Meet--
Face to Face.
Be the cue.
Dance a jig—loose your wig--
Walk the wag.

Play that funky music--
shake your tail
sail your boat
spread your wings
Enter the art--
Gape, Vibe, Jive.

End your journey
as a hero--
Call off the search.
Always seeking, looking--
Be done---
If it pleases you
be true to yourself...
Fold up the maps---
We've found the way
Home!

Choice by Cheryl

Kindness is the border I won't cross.
It is the land I reside in.

Fairness is the foilage---

the trees are strength
they are my family.

I Am a walking tree.
Daughter of Solaris,
Child of Gaia.

Gaia has a new gig,
She will be called the Freedom Wisdom Star.

The old way is done.

Our light will shine the way.

The New Earth, 5D--not 5G--

Join Us--->

Light, Color, Music, Sound...

Vibrations are the bridge---

The Rainbow Bridge.

The codes are in the air, you can feel the change.

Sometimes it's hard to breathe,
All the nonsense; the duality, the tension...
What will we be?

It Is a Choice.

I Want a New Me by Darrel Johannes

Day after day, year after year
the same old me, I wish I would disappear.

The same old thoughts, actions and deeds--
Oh, how I wish I could just be freed.

I often catch a glimpse of the horizon,
the place where what I have been meets eternity.

Could I really leave it, all I have known
and run with fervor to my authentic home.

The place where all misery, strife and pain
would vanish, to less than a memory on a forgotten plain.

I have started my journey, but the price is high
with the only alternative being left to die.

The path is a bit varied for each, I suppose
but the door to our past we all must close.

Life is only here, now in this breath
to ruminate on what was, is certain death.

Our life is made new if we accept the seasons--
Its a miracle of sorts and defies all reason.

Categories kill-- they diminish the mystery.
Our presence is more than facts, logic and history.

Lets catch a wave, take a breath,
allow the spirit its life, in abandon--
Be still, move on, get cleansed
and you will hear it.

We Are One by Cheryl

We are the Many
and We are One.

Flock--
of birds.
Symphony--
of notes.
School--
of fish.
A parade.
Rose garden.
Mandala. Mosaic. Puzzle.
Ant colony.

Deck of cards.
The Multi-Verse---
parallel universes
Stacked
like a deck of cards.

Many of the same thing
same but different.

Like slant rhyme in poetry.
sounds like
but not.

Humanity---
Our similarities and differences
are the same---
Same dramas---
different families.

We are the Many
and We are One.

Souvenirs by Damiel Balderrama

In birth and death,
in growth and decay,
in joy and pain,
the deepest truths are all the same.
We are temporary travelers
upon this physical plane.
The lessons we learn in the flesh
are our souls souvenirs.

Cast Off Children by Cheryl

When I was in the 1st grade
My mom left my dad---
We rode in a Greyhound bus across the country.
I had a little black doll she got me at the giftshop,
and my thumb.

In this society--
when parents get divorced
and remarry
the current family is All.

I didn't even know my dad was in a home.
He passed away yesterday.

RIP
Newel David Hershelman
April 8, 1940 - January 13, 2023

Flex Your Faith by Yuca

The resonance and the power of peace, and of freedom,
is just as contagious as that of fear and chaos.

It's just more difficult for those who've survived in the latter,
to believe and accept the prior.

You will be challenged by unconscious culprits of chaos.
The energy of change is imbued in such challenges, which therein
lack faith.
Those who aren't prepared face faithlessness.
Those of us who are, flex our faith in the face of the faithless,
and prove what it means to walk with God.

The Insurmountable.

Unshakable faith holds the power to turn a coward, into a saint.
I've seen it.
I've done it.
Proof of God is substantially more present than doubt.

Look around, right now.
The level of intelligence is evident.
God is everywhere.

Scrabble **by Cheryl**

Dig up the runes---
the hex dings--

Oy, Er, Aye

Traces of love---
A wife near gone.

Quit putting the cat down.
I never wanted that--
Bless it, with your wand
instead.

Own your hex,
love your warts.

Blue runes
fill the vale with storms.

I loved my near wife
now,
she lives in a zoo,
free of pain.

RIP
John Samuel Hiller
June 19, 1945 - July 4, 2021

1963 by Cheryl
(On the spring equinox at this beach picnic a new life was created.)

I met a girl
on the dock of the bay---
We went on a boat ride,
All afternoon.

She was just a kid,
but I loved her so.

We camped in a patch of green--
next to the beach.

I gave her gin--
she gave me pie.

Follow the cue--
Ja Ja girl.

Say yes to fun--
leave your cave.

Become your own adventure.

Stockholm Syndrome by Cheryl

*Forward that this is a commentary about belief systems,
and it was brought to my attention that some beliefs are
positive, not referring to those.*

Notice the word belief has a lie in it.
Believe the lie.
Live the lie.

There's a difference between
Knowing and Believing---
----(Knowing is Divine)----
Belief is a system of control---
a safety net---

We are being held captive
by belief systems.

Our beliefs are a trap
to control
our every thought and action.

Kidnapped.
Do you love your captor?
Stockholm Syndrome.

Our beliefs---
lies that hold us down.

Small human---
Dependent on--
Technology--
transportation, housing, food.
Systems--
economic, medical, governmental.
Systems of control.

Leave the lies of belief.
Become free.
Free of story, mind and body.

Free your soul.

Where Dreams Come True by Cheryl

On the Merry-Go-Round of Life---
Up and Down,
Round and Round

Here we go---

Take a Leap--
Dive deep--

Hold your breath--
Squeeze your eyes--
shut tight--

Jump
down the wormhole---

To the rainbow
play with Peter Pan--
in Never Never Land.

On the Merry-Go-Round of Life---
I'm gonna ride
all nite long.

The strong wind blows--
to the rainbow--
where dreams come true.

Catch
the next train to Georgia---
Follow the birds
Fly south for the winter.

Past the smog--
You'll find a city in the sky--
Never Never Land

Where dreams come true.

Have you lost your way?
Shut your eyes--
hold your breath--

Pull the plug
go down the drain.
Ride the wind

Round and Round
We go
On the Merry-Go-Round of Life.

To Snow White from Your Prince by anonymous

You are beautiful.
Your voice is like the gentle tap of a spoon
    on an empty champagne glass.
Your eyes sparkle like a huge diamond
    held
to confront the strong, gleaming sun.
Your skin is as a juicy peach, so smooth and sweet
    at its ripest point.
Your lips are like a bloody, rose red
    not some dull, ugly faded red.
Beautiful is your luscious, brown hair as it sways in the wind
    like a vast ocean of prairie grass.
Your touch is like a feather gliding across whoever you touch.
Your smile is like an evil, passing glare of the devil,
    but far from being evil, it is seducing and beautiful.
Your words flow softly, like those of an old, caring woman.
Your mind is strong, you can defeat anyone you please
    yet your body is fragile like glass.
Your looks are your defense.

Birds by Uncle Chester

Birds, birds--in the sky,
look how beautiful--they do fly,
they fly and fly, those beautiful birds in the sky

Although there are many kinds
they must have very humb e minds
for they never seem
to quarrel or fight.

Even tho there are many kinds,
sometimes they seem to say
why can't you be as gay?

Some day we'll be just as gay--
In God's new world
to sing and play.
To my knowledge, I think--
that this is not so far away.
Then we'll hear those birds
and understand their beautiful words.

Orbs by Vylah Daseoc

Oh you orb you lovely being
You absorb her life you give her meaning
So beautiful, all different shapes and sizes so colorful
taking on different disguises
We see you there above her head
You give her life you give her meaning
Vomiting your glittery puke all over her dress, she dances more
the violent gore of violety explosion
So simple and around but so alive you multiply by her sounds
she gives you life she gives you meaning

You are alive by positive energy you feed on good and eat only
good feelings and as she dances the light expands into an
array of floating beings

Winter Eulogy by Robin Houghton

Raven's claw, rabbit's tail
Spruce tree frosted full of quail
Blue jay days, coyote nights
with an ocean spray of lights
Trees are bowing, bears a'napping
Icy winds for snow peaks'capping
Seasons turning, home fires burning
Earth is Resting
Nature, Nesting

Secret Garden by Cheryl

In Oz,
Dorothy
was looking for a way back home---
A spell, talisman, or the wizard.

What did she learn
on her journey?
The wizard could not
give her
what she already had.

Don't Forget
the ancient magic---
We all carry.
You take your wand
where ever you go.

We each have
a Secret Garden---
There,
You can
Access your hidden magic.
Hear the elemental song.

Meet with fairies and pixies.
Sit in circle with Sasquatch.
Listen to the flowers.
The shine of a sparkling creek---
carries the wisdom of the ages.
      Our guides
      direct our path
      and protect us along our way.
In my garden
      the Unicorns stand guard---
      only the pure of heart may enter.
We all have a guardian angel---
      Fairy
      Unicorn
      Dragon
50   Crystal

        Tree or
        Crow,
as unique as we are.

Like the fireflies
they offer light---
Serve as guideposts along the way.

Dorothy
went on a journey
to learn about magic.
Find her way home.
By helping others
she found her way.

This path---Elusive
Can not be forced.
Can not be captured, bottled or sold.
You can find it---
In the wisdom of the owl
Fire of a dragon
Flight of a fairy
And from the strength of unicorns.

They say---
"It's not the destination, but the journey."
This one rings true.

At any time
We feel lost
We can visit
our own
Secret Garden---
where we have many helpers.
They are patient
guiding us
Until
we Remember
our power---
and find our way home
like Dorothy did.

Water by Heather Brook

Water, a timeless essence,
An ancient memory it holds,
Its holy frequencies, so dense,
An elixir, so bold.

In every drop, a story untold,
Of the Earth and its creation,
Of civilizations, young and old,
And their preservation.

It flows through mountains high,
And deserts, so vast and bare,
It touches every living being,
And in every soul, it does repair.

Water, the sacred elixir,
That nourishes our earthly form,
In its holy vibrations,
Our bodies are forever reborn.

For water is life, and life is love,
An eternal dance of birth and death,
And in its depths, the secrets of the universe,
Are waiting to be unlocked with every breath.

So, let us listen to the whispers of the water,
And feel its holy frequencies, so divine,
For in its memory, the answers we do seek,
To our purpose, and the meaning of life's design.

Mutation by Robin Houghton

I live large,
in compartmentalized splendor,
80 feet from a pond,
  a water-world
   abundant
  with red-wing blackbirds,
  occasional ducks and geese,
    cattails, brambles,
     and FROGS--
     lots of frogs:
   bull frogs & tree frogs,
   big frogs and little frogs,
Croaking loudly, softly,
   daily, nightly,
And in the midst of this
  treasure of symphonic bio-diversity
  I seem to have discovered
   a new and strange
-- dare I say mutant --
  amphibian life-form:
    the WHEATGRASS FROG!

These Marco Polos of the pond world
  inexplicably hop forth,
   through wooded verge and curried lawn,
  o'er hedge and under odd imperative,
To reach the gray and unassuming wall
  of my apartment building,
   and thence to climb,
    suctioned foot-by-foot,
   to my second-story turrret...

There in a mini-greenhouse is my
wheatgrass,
   growing greenly,
  blissfully unaware of its alter-ego
  as the Shangri-La of a bunch of
    demented mutant frogs.
Without enough sense to enjoy life in the
pond!

And so my porch is subject
  to sudden random fits
    of croaks & other
      startling froggy noises--
Perhaps alerting other amphibian oddballs
  of this rare, even spiritual opportunity?

I've certainly learned somewhat about frogs:
  for instance, they can fly,
   -- mostly horizontal --
    for about 30 feet,
   land in the grass,
  and be perfectly all right (apparently),
If they're given a bit of a boost.
Also, the silly buggers
pee all over you when you grab 'em,
  just like toads.

How these creatures know
 -- and why they care --
  that trays of wheat are growing
   80 feet away and 20 feet above them
Is the Mystery that really *gets me most*!

  After all --
Any fool can teach a frog to fly
But only Spirit knows
   the What & Why!
So now I let the froggies come and go
-- I've learned that life is more than
   peace and quiet--
For Everything is Sacred,
  dont'cha know,
And frog's-legs are no longer
  In my diet!!

Samuel, a very small fish by Shamballa

Samuel was a small fish in the big sea, but he could swim deep, deep, deep. And he swam so free. His eyes on either side were open so wide to take in all that he did survey. Samuel was amazed at all the different life forms in the sea, he loved seeing the jellyfish like ballerinas moving so effortlessly. He was afraid of the big fish that might eat him so he would hide in little crevices of beautiful colored coral and shells. But Samuel loved most of all the mermaids. And though they were rare, he knew one lair where they did live. He would go just at a distance not to let them know and he would watch how they brushed their hair and giggled among them selves and had these objects that they looked upon them selves with. He was fascinated and when they would sing Samuel's whole body would ring.

Well, one day Samuel was swimming in the sea and a bigger fish caught him. But it was not as he thought it would be, as the fish swallowed him and he dissolved. He felt he was now part of the fish looking through his eyes, observing all the sea. It was still him, watching and learning, and enjoying the swim.

Ahhh, this fish was a Dolphin, a mammal fish you see that had eaten Samuel as he swam. The Dolphin was rising to the surface fast, exhilarating Samuel, and he would leap. Oh, the Sun was a new thing to Samuel. He loved it when the Dolphin would leap and spin and oh the warm rays of the Sun touching his body, glistening on his own skin. And fell into the water, again and again. Oh such fun to be the Dolphin, now you see. The dolphins in groups swam the great sea, so close, in higher mind communicating all the time as they grazed each others bodies playfully. This was also new for Samuel, singing, talking and making love. Celebrating Life, jumping into the sky and sun. Oh, what fun! This was awesome! This was great! Samuel loved swimming in waves and curves and straights. And, by the seashore where he leaped, surfed and saw creatures now. They walked it seemed, standing upright, the opposite of him, in their being. How weird they looked and multi-color too. Samuel loved jumping near the shore to see this thing so new. Oh my goodness, what a world in which he was! The sea and air and Sun.

One day Samuel was swimming with his pod, leaping up and down. But this time when he leaped, there was no Sun. There was water falling from the sky, as far as he could see, little drops. Each splash made a note, thrilling his every cell. What a delight, as he twisted and turned to learn,yes, Samuel did flow with it all, letting go. What a wonder, being a dolphin in the sea. One time, sharks came, but his dolphin friends came and chased them away! Ahhh, being in a group had its way.

Oh they swam the sea, shores and deep, living life in joy and ecstacy. Samuel wanted to share this joy with all he could see. He tried to sing it. He tried to let them know of Love To Be...

55

Treasure Hunt by Cheryl

Do you have a broken heart?

Rescue the shards of your heart.
They are treasure.

Search and Rescue.

What is hiding
down
In the
basement of your heart?

Go inward--
to the ward of your heart.

Go deep--dive
to the depths
of your soul.

Dive for treasure.
Treasure Hunt.

Go deep
into the
abyss of nothing.

Enter the Void--

The Black Hole
of complete emptiness.

Only then,
        can you
Run
with your wild horses.
56

Don't worry---You won't get lost.
Follow
the white rabbit.
She knows the way.

Many thanks to these contributors:

Damiel Balderrama
Heather Brook
Uncle Chester
Vylah Daseoc
Jennifer Hershelman
Robin Houghton
Darrel Johannes
Cody Ray Richardson
Crystal Scarlett
Shamballa
Yeshardo
Yuca
and the anonymous poet

About the author---

Cheryl Lunar Wind lives in the Mount Shasta area in a little town called Weed. She is a practicer of Mayan cosmology, Lakota ceremony, Star Knowledge and the Universal Laws including the Law of One. Her hobbies are writing poetry, music, dance, drum circles and love for all life; plant, animal and crystal. Cheryl has been a guide and spiritual teacher for many years. Now she shares wisdom and wit through poetry, and has published poetry books; Know Your Way, We Are One and Follow the White Rabbit.

Testimonials---

"Cheryl's words work magic in my heart, stirring the wisdom that is buried so deeply within me---beautiful indeed!"
Ellie Pfeiffer, founder of Ellie's Espresso & Bakery, Weed, CA

"Cheryl's poetry is very inspiring--particularly the way she compares life with the forces of nature. There is a special element in her poems that opens my heart and fills my soul with divine possibilities."
Giovanna Taormina, Co-Founder, One Circle Foundation

"Cheryl's poems have helped me to uncover and honor my own hidden memories. The beauty of her spirit is evident in each tender, insightful passage."
Marguerite Lorimer, www.earthalive.com